Success
Assessment Papers

Verbal
Reasoning
age 9–10

Alison Primrose

Sample page

example at the beginning of
each section of questions

paper number for
quick reference

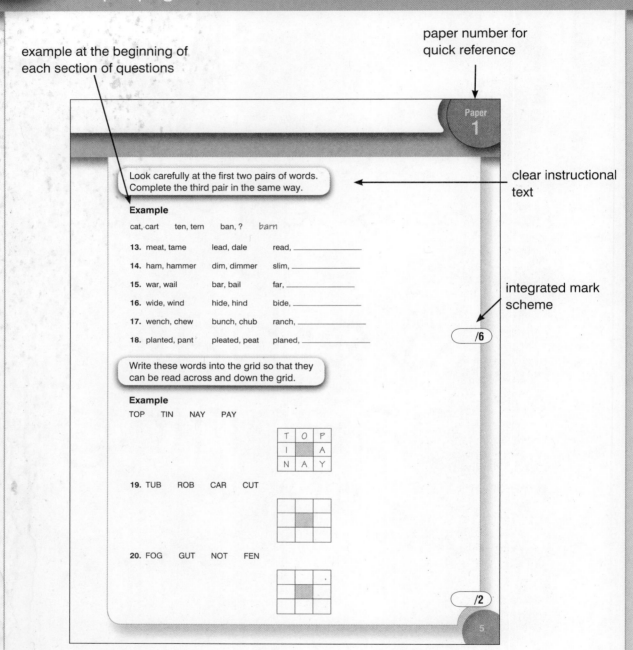

Paper
1

Look carefully at the first two pairs of words.
Complete the third pair in the same way.

clear instructional
text

Example

cat, cart   ten, tern   ban, ?   barn

13. meat, tame   lead, dale   read, _____

14. ham, hammer   dim, dimmer   slim, _____

15. war, wail   bar, bail   far, _____

16. wide, wind   hide, hind   bide, _____

17. wench, chew   bunch, chub   ranch, _____

18. planted, pant   pleated, peat   planed, _____

integrated mark
scheme

/6

Write these words into the grid so that they
can be read across and down the grid.

Example

TOP   TIN   NAY   PAY

T	O	P
I		A
N	A	Y

19. TUB   ROB   CAR   CUT

20. FOG   GUT   NOT   FEN

/2

5

Contents

PAPER 1

In each group of five words below, there are three words that go together in some way. Identify the two words that **do not** belong to the group and underline them.

Example

cat   cockerel   donkey   camel   python

1. March   Monday   April   June   Summer

2. parrot   hedgehog   sparrow   hawk   fox

3. strawberry   oats   barley   straw   wheat

4. spectacles   telescope   mirror   magnet   microscope

5. calm   turbulent   peaceful   placid   chaotic

6. slow   fast   rapid   minute   swift

/6

In each sentence below, the word in capitals has three letters missing. The missing letters make a proper three-letter word on their own. Write the three-letter word.

Example

She spread the sweet HY on her toast.   ONE

7. They packed their bags for the long JNEY. _____

8. Her favourite chocolate was DY milk. _____

9. Using the COMER, he sent a message to his friend in Spain. _____

10. SUDLY there was a bright flash of light! _____

11. They gazed at the wonderful PAINGS in the gallery. _____

12. The new loaves were set out on the BREADBD. _____

/6

Look carefully at the first two pairs of words.
Complete the third pair in the same way.

Example

cat, cart   ten, tern   ban, ?   *barn*

13. meat, tame   lead, dale   read, _____

14. ham, hammer   dim, dimmer   slim, _____

15. war, wail   bar, bail   far, _____

16. wide, wind   hide, hind   bide, _____

17. wench, chew   bunch, chub   ranch, _____

18. planted, pant   pleated, peat   planed, _____

/6

Write these words into the grid so that they
can be read across and down the grid.

Example

TOP   TIN   NAY   PAY

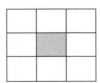

19. TUB   ROB   CAR   CUT

20. FOG   GUT   NOT   FEN

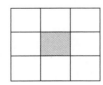

/2

Choose two words, one from each set of brackets, so that the second pair of words is completed in the same way as the first pair. Underline the words.

Example

Cow is to (milk, <u>calf</u>, herd) as horse is to (jump, saddle, <u>foal</u>).

21. Cup is to (mug, saucer, plate) as knife is to (spoon, cut, fork).

22. Early is to (sunrise, punctual, late) as morning is to (dark, evening, breakfast).

23. Snow is to (white, cold, fun) as grass is to (park, picnic, green).

24. Sleeve is to (cover, cuff, arm) as collar is to (shirt, neck, button).

25. Agriculture is to (tractor, farming, potatoes) as horticulture is to (gardening, weeds, patio).

26. Hot is to (chocolate, steam, cold) and tall is to (narrow, short, lanky).

/6

Move one letter from the first word and add it to the second word to make two new, correctly spelt words. The order of the letters **cannot** be changed.

Example

plain   pad   →   <u>plan</u>   <u>paid</u>

27. string   cash → _____   _____

28. bead   fed → _____   _____

29. wring   don → _____   _____

30. bread   lend → _____   _____

31. beat   mat → _____   _____

32. boulder   clod → _____   _____

/6

Substitute the values for the letters and work out these equations. Give each answer as a letter.

Example

If A = 2, B = 5, C = 8, D = 12 and E = 20, what is the value of A × E ÷ C = ?   B̲

If A = 3, B = 4, C = 8, D = 31 and E = 24, what is the value of:

33. A + B + E = _____

34. E − C ÷ B = _____

35. B × C − D + A = _____

If A = 15, B = 12, C = 2, D = 5 and E = 25, what is the value of:

36. C × D + A = _____

37. A − B × D = _____

38. E − A + C = _____

/6

Which of the following words **cannot** be made from the letters of the word in capitals? Underline the word.

Example

| STATIONERY | state | stone | t̲o̲w̲n̲s̲ | notes | train |

39. NATURE   tare   tune   near   treat   true

40. METALLIC   came   lilt   calm   colt   lace

41. SPREAD   pear   drips   dares   ears   drapes

42. FIREWORK   wire   fork   fried   rower   weir

43. DINOSAUR   sound   rind   sand   sauna   ruin

44. EQUATOR   tare   quote   quart   true   equate

/6

Remove one letter from the word in capitals to leave a new word. The meaning of the new word is given in the clue.

Example

WANT   an insect   <u>ANT</u>

45. FOLDER   not younger   _____

46. BRUSHES   shrubs   _____

47. MENTAL   usually magnetic _____

48. PATIENT   shiny black   _____

49. WIELD   join metal   _____

50. BRANCH   very large farm   _____

/6

/50

PAPER 2

In each group of five words below, there are three words that go together in some way. Identify the two words that **do not** belong to the group and underline them.

Example

cat   <u>cockerel</u>   donkey   camel   python

1. cube   cuboid   triangle   prism   circle

2. sticky   glossy   gluey   shiny   gleaming

3. opera   orchestra   concerto   sonata   quartet

4. wealthy   miser   rich   pauper   affluent

5. sapphire   diamond   gold   emerald   silver

6. almond   walnut   marzipan   sultana   cashew

/6

Look carefully at these letter sequences. Work out the patterns to find the next letters in the sequence. The alphabet is here to help you.

A B C D E F G H I J K L M N O P Q R S T U V W X Y Z

Example

AB   DE   GH   JK   ?   MN

7. AC   DF   GI   JL   _____

8. ZX   VT   RP   NL   _____

9. AD   CF   EH   GJ   _____

10. NM   NO   LK   PQ   _____

11. AP   BQ   CR   DS   _____

12. ZY   AC   XW   EG   _____

/6

Substitute the values for the letters and work out these equations. Give each answer as a letter.

Example

If A = 2, B = 5, C = 8, D = 12 and E = 20, what is the value of $A \times E \div C = ?$ B

If A = 20, B = 2, C = 5, D = 30 and E = 4, what is the value of:

13. $C \times B + A =$ _____

14. $D + A \div B - C =$ _____

15. $C \times E \times B - A =$ _____

If A = 5, B = 12, C = 17, D = 4 and E = 3, what is the value of:

16. $D \times A - E =$ _____

17. $C - A \div D =$ _____

/6

18. $B - A + E + D + E =$ _____

Rearrange the capital letters to form a correctly spelt word that will complete these sentences sensibly. Write the word on the answer line.

Example

She led the horse to the ABTESL.   STABLE

19. The children were looking forward to the OHIYDSAL. _____

20. A lovely smell was wafting out of the TIKEHNC. _____

21. It was a UATIFEULB bunch of flowers! _____

22. He chose a slice of the chocolate AGEUTA. _____

23. There was a ADGENBA on his bad leg. _____

24. The TEMURPT played a loud fanfare. _____

/6

Look carefully at the codes and work out the answers to the questions.

Example

If the code for STEAM is 32415, what does the code 341 stand for?   SEA

If the code for REPEAT is 534321:

25. What does the code 1325 stand for? _____

26. What is the code for PART? _____

27. What does 4325 stand for? _____

If the codes for CAN, CAP and PEN are 453, 213 and 214, but not in that order:

28. What is the code for CAPE? _____

29. What does the code 45325 stand for? _____

30. What is the code for PEEP? _____

/6

Write these words into the grid so that they can be read across and down the grid.

Example

TOP   TIN   NAY   PAY

31. PUP   YAP   TAP   TRY

32. AYE   SEA   TEE   SIT

/2

Move one letter from the first word and add it to the second word to make two new, correctly spelt words. The order of the letters **cannot** be changed.

Example

plain   pad   →   _plan_   _paid_

33. grange   round   →   _____   _____

34. break   cash   →   _____   _____

35. whey   wed   →   _____   _____

36. plump   layer   →   _____   _____

37. frog   bush   →   _____   _____

38. soon   bat   →   _____   _____

/6

In each of these sentences, there is a four-letter word hidden across two words. The letters are in the right order and make a correctly spelt word. Write the word.

Example

It was fis<u>h and</u> chips for supper.   <u>hand</u>

39. The hotel lady welcomed them. _____

40. They went to the last opera of the season. _____

41. They got together at coffee time. _____

42. The train was very late arriving. _____

43. The girls often met up together. _____

44. The alarm made everyone jump. _____

/6

Remove one letter from the word in capitals to leave a new word. The meaning of the new word is given in the clue.

Example

WANT   an insect   <u>ANT</u>

45. COAST   price   _____

46. SCENT   coin   _____

47. PIRATE   angry   _____

48. BREADTH   gulp of air   _____

49. BLANK   grassy slope   _____

50. TITLE   ceramic square   _____

/6

/50

PAPER 3

Look carefully at the codes and work out the answers to the questions.

Example

If the code for STEAM is 32415, what does the code 341 stand for?   <u>SEA</u>

If the code for ENTERED is 4124345:

   1. What does the code 5443 stand for? _____

   2. What is the code for TEN? _____

   3. What does the code 3412 stand for? _____

If the codes for TEN, SON and NOT are 246, 136 and 641, but not in that order:

   4. What is the code for STONE? _____

   5. What is 6321 the code for? _____

   6. What is the code for SENSE? _____

/6

In each sentence below, the word in capitals has three letters missing. The missing letters make a proper three-letter word on their own. Write the three-letter word.

Example

She spread the sweet HY on her toast.   <u>ONE</u>

   7. The CROILES were motionless. _____

   8. They all went to the party in CY dress. _____

   9. The JAESE ladies wore kimonos. _____

  10. The children held the SPLERS carefully. _____

  11. They made CNEY with all the apples. _____

  12. He won the photography COMITION. _____

/6

Look carefully at the first two pairs of words.
Complete the third pair in the same way.

Example

cat, cart   ten, tern   ban, ?   <u>barn</u>

13. rope, room   bone, boom   dose, _____

14. wrench, bench   wreck, beck   write, _____

15. flip, flap   tip, tap   trip, _____

16. fare, fair   hare, hair   pare, _____

17. bid, binder   wad, wander   fed, _____

18. lace, lack   pace, pack   race, _____

/6

Look carefully at these letter sequences. Work out the patterns to find
the next letters in each sequence. The alphabet is here to help you.

A B C D E F G H I J K L M N O P Q R S T U V W X Y Z

Example

AB   DE   GH   JK   ?   <u>MN</u>

19. AZ   BY   CX   DW   _____

20. BD   FH   JL   NP   _____

21. YW   US   QO   MK   _____

22. PN   QM   RL   SK   _____

23. ZW   YX   VS   UT   RO   _____

24. EA   FB   GC   HD   _____

/6

Which of the following words **cannot** be made from the letters of the word in capitals? Underline the word.

Example

STATIONERY   state   stone   <u>towns</u>   notes   train

25. ADVENTURE   vane   true   toad   veer   rude

26. SOLSTICE   lice   list   toss   still   coil

27. RECIPE   peer   rice   pear   price   piece

28. LIBRARIAN   bail   brain   nail   barrel   aria

29. RECEPTION   note   creep   pint   optic   peace

30. MACHINE   name   inch   mean   ranch   chain

/6

Write these words into the grid so that they can be read across and down the grid.

Example

TOP   TIN   NAY   PAY

T	O	P
I		A
N	A	Y

31. WIN   NEW   WIT   TOW

32. LIT   POP   LAP   TIP

/2

Choose two words, one from each set of brackets, so that the second pair of words is completed in the same way as the first pair. Underline the words.

Example

Cow is to (milk, <u>calf,</u> herd) as horse is to (jump, saddle, <u>foal</u>).

33. Circle is to (pentagon, square, oval) as sphere is to (pyramid, cube, prism).

34. Lion is to (mane, roar, cub) as cat is to (kitten, milk, basket).

35. Bird is to (feathers, nest, egg) as fish is to (water, scales, chips).

36. Kilometre is to (run, distance, mile) as kilogram is to (mass, scales, litre).

37. Paint is to (palette, brush, canvas) as ink is to (blot, writing, pen).

38. Sugar is to (candy, cane, sweet) as lemon is to (sour, juice, yellow).

/6

In each of these sentences, there is a four-letter word hidden across two words. The letters are in the right order and make a correctly spelt word. Write the word.

Example

It was fi<u>sh and</u> chips for supper.   <u>hand</u>

39. The post arrived late today. _____

40. She put tinsel over the picture. _____

41. He had to wait for ages. _____

42. The presents were all ready. _____

43. There was half a bottle left. _____

44. The big window needed cleaning. _____

/6

Rearrange the capital letters to form a correctly spelt word that will complete these sentences sensibly. Write the word on the answer line.

Example

She led the horse to the ABTESL.   <u>STABLE</u>

45. On Shrove Tuesday, they ate KAEPNASC. _____

46. They went to the NIECAM to see their favourite film. _____

47. They were tired after the long EONYJUR. _____

48. The NIALMAS were very tame. _____

49. Many cars were stranded in the LABIZRZD. _____

50. The tomato plants grew in the ORESENGHUE. _____

/6

/50

PAPER 4

Write these words into the grid so that they can be read across and down the grid.

Example

TOP   TIN   NAY   PAY

1. PIN   MOP   MAT   TEN

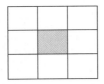

2. DAY   YES   BUS   DAB

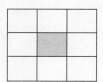

In each group of five words below, there are three words that go together in some way. Identify the two words that **do not** belong to the group and underline them.

Example

cat   <u>cockerel</u>   donkey   camel   <u>python</u>

3. shiny   sparkly   dusty   glittery   frosty

4. cruiser   mansion   cottage yacht   liner

5. chestnut   toffee   hazel   almond   treacle

6. mountain   valley   dale   hill   alp

7. mug   plate   cup   tumbler   saucer

8. puppy   leveret   ewe   foal   mare

/6

Choose two words, one from each set of brackets, so that the second pair of words is completed in the same way as the first pair. Underline the words.

Example

Cow is to (milk, <u>calf,</u> herd) as horse is to (jump, saddle, <u>foal</u>).

9. Snow is to (white, flake, cold) as rain is to (umbrella, cloud, drop).

10. Bread is to (loaf, sandwich, crust) as flowers are to (colour, daisies, bunch).

11. Turquoise is to (river, blue, colour) as crimson is to (berries, red, blood).

12. Book is to (author, novel, biography) as symphony is to (concert, composer, film).

13. Notes are to (music, orchestra, singing) as letters are to (alphabet, reading, capitals).

14. Light is to (day, dark, candle) as wet is to (cold, damp, dry).

/6

In each of these sentences, there is a four-letter word hidden across two words. The letters are in the right order and make a correctly spelt word. Write the word.

Example

It was fish and chips for supper.   <u>hand</u>

15. The tribe arrived late that night. _____

16. Last time altogether now! _____

17. The old camel tottered to her feet. _____

18. Please drop everything and come quickly. _____

19. I have stopped the payments. _____

20. We have time to build one more tower. _____

/6

Remove one letter from the word in capitals to leave a new word. The meaning of the new word is given in the clue.

Example

WANT   an insect   <u>ANT</u>

21. CROCKERY   stony border   _____

22. PLEDGES   narrow shelves   _____

23. REVOLVE   develop from   _____

24. WITCH   irritation   _____

25. LINEAR   large ship   _____

26. PLAICE   location   _____

/6

19

Substitute the values for the letters and work out these equations. Give each answer as a letter.

Example

If A = 2, B = 5, C = 8, D = 12 and E = 20, what is the value of A × E ÷ C = ?   <u>B</u>

If A = 3, B = 6, C = 16, D = 2 and E = 24, what is the value of:

27. B × A + B = _____

28. E ÷ A × D = _____

29. E + B ÷ A + B = _____

If A = 5, B = 20, C = 3, D = 12 and E = 4, what is the value of:

30. B ÷ A × C = _____

31. B × C ÷ D = _____

32. D × E − B − C ÷ A = _____

/6

Move one letter from the first word and add it to the second word to make two new, correctly spelt words. The order of the letters **cannot** be changed.

Example

plain   pad   →   <u>plan</u>   <u>paid</u>

33. warm   pal   →   _____   _____

34. frill   dip   →   _____   _____

35. moist   pen   →   _____   _____

36. scamp   pies   →   _____   _____

37. flatter   pot   →   _____   _____

38. bread   ranch   →   _____   _____

/6

Look carefully at these letter sequences. Work out the patterns to find the next letters in each sequence. The alphabet is here to help you.

A B C D E F G H I J K L M N O P Q R S T U V W X Y Z

Example

AB   DE   GH   JK   ?   <u>MN</u>

39. KJ   ML   ON   QP   _____

40. ZA   BX   VC   DT   _____

41. BD   CE   DF   EG   _____

42. ZY   VU   RQ   NM   _____

43. FG   HJ   KN   OS   _____

44. FW   VE   DU   TC   _____

/6

Which of the following words **cannot** be made from the letters of the word in capitals? Underline the word.

Example

STATIONERY   state   stone   <u>towns</u>   notes   train

45. ROTATION   toot   rotor   tart   taint   train

46. BEEFBURGER   urge   grub   beer   green   free

47. MARRIAGE   rage   game   germ   garage   grime

48. COUNTERPANE   canter   pact   crate   preen   tenet

49. MASQUERADE   quad   square   dram   dames   squid

/6

50. TRANSITION   train   saint   stone   strain   nation

/50

PAPER 5

In each group of five words below, there are three words that go together in some way. Identify the two words that **do not** belong to the group and underline them.

Example

cat   <u>cockerel</u>   donkey   camel   <u>python</u>

1. steps   stairs   path   ladder   track

2. waste   refuse   rubbish   tins   compost

3. legend   programme   poster   tale   story

4. display   competition   exhibit   show   sell

5. discount   cheap   reduction   bargain   deduction

6. carry   give   clutch   grasp   take

/6

Look carefully at the given codes and work out the answers to the questions.

Example

If the code for STEAM is 32415, what does the code 341 stand for?   <u>SEA</u>

If the code for THEATRE is 3521342:

7. What is the code for RATE? _____

8. What does the code 34213 stand for? _____

9. What is the code for EARTH? _____

If the codes for BEG, GOT and BAT are 134, 425 and 165:

10. What is the code for GOAT? _____

11. What does the code 1365 stand for? _____

12. What is the code for TOGA? _____

/6

Move one letter from the first word and add it to the second word to make two new, correctly spelt words. The order of the letters **cannot** be changed.

Example

plain   pad → <u>plan</u>   <u>paid</u>

13. strain   tip   →   _____   _____

14. whopper   hen   →   _____   _____

15. smile   pans   →   _____   _____

16. grate   rim   →   _____   _____

17. blush   pod   →   _____   _____

18. plant   wan   →   _____   _____

/6

Look carefully at the first two pairs of words. Complete the third pair in the same way.

Example

cat, cart   ten, tern   ban, ?   <u>barn</u>

19. bunny, buy   bucket, but   panel, _____

20. fresher, fresh   cooker, cook   dealer, _____

21. carriage, cage   present, pent   selections, _____

22. meadow, dame   leather, tale   measure, _____

23. wood, would   buy, bye   here, _____

24. plant, planet   shard, shared   wand, _____

/6

23

Look carefully at these letter sequences. Work out the patterns to find the next letters in each sequence. The alphabet is here to help you.

A B C D E F G H I J K L M N O P Q R S T U V W X Y Z

Example

AB   DE   GH   JK   ?   <u>MN</u>

25. KL   NO   QR   TU   _____

26. CE   FD   GI   JH   _____

27. AO   BP   CQ   DR   _____

28. WV   SR   ON   KJ   _____

29. BZ   AY   ZX   YW   _____

30. HZ   WH   HT   QH   _____

/6

Write these words into the grid so that they can be read across and down the grid.

Example

TOP   TIN   NAY   PAY

T	O	P
I		A
N	A	Y

31. TUB   BOA   TAB   BAA

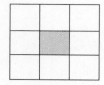

32. MAN   GET   NET   MUG

/2

In each sentence below, the word in capitals has three letters missing. The missing letters make a proper three-letter word on their own. Write the three-letter word.

Example

She spread the sweet HY on her toast.   <u>ONE</u>

33. The picture was MAGIC and stuck to the fridge door. _____

34. You could hear the TPET player clearly. _____

35. The grape juice is allowed to FERT to make wine. _____

36. He loved GEOGHY lessons, learning about different countries. _____

37. The flower ARGEMENT was quite stunning. _____

38. The old lady had a yellow ARY. _____

/6

Remove one letter from the word in capitals to leave a new word. The meaning of the new word is given in the clue.

Example

WANT   an insect   <u>ANT</u>

39. CHANCEL   to put off   _____

40. COUNTRY   a region or part of a country   _____

41. DANGER   wrath   _____

42. PETAL   a ringing of bells   _____

43. PINCH   measurement   _____

44. TAINT   colour shade   _____

/6

25

Rearrange the capital letters to form a correctly spelt word that will complete these sentences sensibly. Write the word on the answer line.

Example

She led the horse to the ABTESL. ___STABLE___

45. They flew down the snowy slope on the AOGNTGOB. _____

46. Everyday the HERNILCD visited the farm next door. _____

47. They met at the MENCIA to see the new film. _____

48. They all had a great time in the EASENMUTM park. _____

49. The family got together to celebrate their SARYNIARVEN. _____

50. His picture was displayed at the EOTIXBIHIN in the town. _____

/6

/50

PAPER 6

Look carefully at the given codes and work out the answers to the questions.

Example

If the code for STEAM is 32415, what does the code 341 stand for? ___SEA___

If the code for LITTLER is 4133425:

1. What is the code for TILL? _____

2. What does the code 3522 represent? _____

3. What is the code for TIER? _____

If the codes for TEN, SEA and ATE are 125, 542 and 423, but not in that order:

4. What is the code for ANT? _____

5. What does the code 154 represent? _____

6. What is the code for TEASE? _____

/6

Choose two words, one from each set of brackets, so that the second pair of words is completed in the same way as the first pair. Underline the words.

Example

Cow is to (milk, calf, herd) as horse is to (jump, saddle, foal).

7. Slow is to (worm, fast, late) as wide is to (broad, narrow, fat).

8. Pillow is to (sleep, kitten, bed) as cushion is to (chair, comfortable, pins).

9. Knife is to (cut, dinner, fork) as salt is to (pepper, spice, grain).

10. Sock is to (shoe, warm, colour) as collar is to (smart, tie, formal).

11. Shallow is to (paddle, fish, deep) as high is to (tide, low, moon).

12. Ascend is to (climb, mountain, descend) as rise is to (sun, fall, float).

/6

In each of these sentences, there is a four-letter word hidden across two words. The letters are in the right order and make a correctly spelt word. Write the word.

Example

It was fish and chips for supper.   hand

13. The view is best early in the morning. _____

14. When shall we three meet again? _____

15. The children took presents to the party. _____

16. They played cat and mouse all day! _____

17. The damsel flies hovered by the pond. _____

18. He leaned over the barrier to get the book. _____

/6

Look carefully at the first two pairs of words.
Complete the third pair in the same way.

Example

cat, cart   ten, tern   ban, ?   <u>barn</u>

19. wish, dish   ware, dare   wry, _____

20. brown, brow   drawn, draw   crown, _____

21. fell, felt   mall, malt   till, _____

22. game, age   lame, ale   came, _____

23. fin, find   win, wind   bin, _____

24. fate, father,   gate, gather,   rate, _____

/6

Which of the following words **cannot** be made from the letters
of the word in capitals? Underline the word.

Example

STATIONERY	state	stone	<u>towns</u>	notes	train

25. MANAGER	mane	anger	game	ream	groan
26. NOTELET	note	tell	teen	tone	lent
27. RIVIERA	river	rave	view	arrive	rare
28. PLEASANT	plant	stale	planet	pleat	apple
29. BENEATH	tenth	bent	bath	bean	than
30. WHITHER	white	hew	their	writhe	trite

/6

Write these words into the grid so that they can be read across and down the grid.

Example

TOP   TIN   NAY   PAY

31. DAY   BUY   FIB   FAD

32. WAS   TOW   SAW   WIT

/2

In each sentence below, the word in capitals has three letters missing. The missing letters make a proper three-letter word on their own. Write the three-letter word.

Example

She spread the sweet HY on her toast.   <u>ONE</u>

33. The WE roses had a wonderful perfume. _____

34. They went at a TER across the open moors. _____

35. He loved the new COMER game. _____

36. She signed the important DOCUT straight away. _____

37. The leaves were all BLOG in the wind. _____

/6

38. The SNY horse was very hungry. _____

Substitute the values for the letters and work out these equations. Give each answer as a letter.

Example

If A = 2, B = 5, C = 8, D = 12 and E = 20, what is the value of A × E ÷ C = ?   <u>B</u>

If A = 4, B = 8, C = 10, D = 15 and E = 5, what is the value of:

39. C + D ÷ E = _____

40. A × C ÷ E = _____

41. D ÷ E × C − D = _____

If A = 3, B = 4, C = 7, D = 14 and E = 21, what is the value of:

42. B × C − D = _____

43. E ÷ A + B + A + C = _____

44. D × A − E − C = _____

/6

Rearrange the capital letters to form a correctly spelt word that will complete these sentences sensibly. Write the word on the answer line.

Example

She led the horse to the ABTESL.   <u>STABLE</u>

45. The old lady's garden was like a MOWDEA! _____

46. The SINILMOUE drew up and they were driven to the party. _____

47. The old FRYTOAC chimneys were demolished. _____

48. The photographs brought back many happy MOESMERI. _____

49. The manager was a very WAYLTEH man. _____

/6

50. They received their ECECAFITRTIS at the Prizegiving. _____

/50

PAPER 7

In each group of five words below, there are three words that go together in some way. Identify the two words that **do not** belong in the group and underline them.

Example

cat   <u>cockerel</u>   donkey   camel   <u>python</u>

1. rain   sunshine   summer   autumn   wind

2. school   university   hospital   college   office

3. necklace   ring   skirt   bracelet   trousers

4. candle   lantern   blinds   curtains   lamp

5. funny   amusing   comical   historical   fictional

6. hockey   snap   tennis   football   swimming

/6

Look carefully at the given codes and work out the answers to the questions.

Example

If the code for STEAM is 32415, what does the code 341 stand for? <u>SEA</u>

If the code for REPEAT is 314125:

7. What is the code for APE? _____

8. What does the code 524 stand for? _____

9. What is the code for PEAR? _____

If the codes for SAW, SEW and WET are 341, 145 and 321, but not in that order:

10. What is the code for TEA? _____

11. What does the code 345 stand for? _____

12. What is the code for STEW? _____

/6

Move one letter from the first word and add it to the second word to make two new, correctly spelt words. The order of the letters **cannot** be changed.

Example

plain   pad → <u>plan</u>   <u>paid</u>

13. wined   pin   →   _____   _____

14. flurry   fame   →   _____   _____

15. plumber   tram   →   _____   _____

16. cost   tones   →   _____   _____

17. break   pawn   →   _____   _____

18. flounder   sea   →   _____   _____

/6

In each of these sentences, there is a four-letter word hidden across two words. The letters are in the right order and make a correctly spelt word. Write the word.

Example

It was fi<u>sh and</u> chips for supper.   <u>hand</u>

19. What a useful little box! _____

20. Please find an early time. _____

21. The rabbits hopped away as we walked along. _____

22. We might need to dip into our savings. _____

23. The ornamental knife was very old. _____

24. The pelican eats a lot of fish each day. _____

/6

Find a three-letter word within the word in capitals, which has the meaning given in the clue.

Example

WANTING   an insect   <u>ANT</u>

25. ANTARCTIC   used for roads   _____

26. CAPITAL   a deep hole   _____

27. MISTLETOE   allow   _____

28. RAILWAY   feel unwell   _____

29. MANUSCRIPT   tear   _____

30. ENTICED   frozen water   _____

/6

Look carefully at these letter sequences. Work out the patterns to find the next letters in each sequence. The alphabet is here to help you.

A B C D E F G H I J K L M N O P Q R S T U V W X Y Z

Example

AB   DE   GH   JK   ?   <u>MN</u>

31. AD   BE   CF   DG   _____

32. ZY   XV   UT   SQ   _____

33. JB   KC   LD   ME   _____

34. BD   FH   JL   NP   _____

35. AA   AB   BD   BG   CK   _____

36. FG   IJ   LM   OP   _____

/6

Substitute the values for the letters and work out these equations. Give each answer as a letter.

Example

If A = 2, B = 5, C = 8, D = 12 and E = 20, what is the value of A × E ÷ C = ? <u>B</u>

If A = 4, B = 3, C = 30, D = 8 and E = 2, what is the value of:

37. C ÷ B − D = _____

38. D × E ÷ A = _____

39. C − D ÷ E + A × E = _____

If A = 32, B = 12, C = 10, D = 2 and E = 8, what is the value of:

40. A − B ÷ D = _____

41. E + B + C + D = _____

42. A ÷ D − E = _____

/6

Write these words into the grid so that they can be read across and down the grid.

Example

TOP   TIN   NAY   PAY

T	O	P
I		A
N	A	Y

43. DAD   MUD   ROD   RUM

44. TOT   VET   NOT   VAN

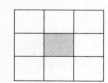

/2

Which of the following words **cannot** be made from the letters of the word in capitals? Underline the word.

Example

STATIONERY   state   stone   <u>towns</u>   notes   train

45.	BALANCE	lance	bale	clan	club	lane
46.	PLATTER	plate	relate	part	treat	pear
47.	SHIELD	shed	hide	sled	dish	lead
48.	FOREST	rest	sore	store	stir	fret
49.	MISCHIEF	chief	mice	fish	mesh	flesh
50.	CANTER	cane	actor	crane	near	race

/6

/50

PAPER 8

In each sentence below, the word in capitals has three letters missing. The missing letters make a proper three-letter word on their own. Write the three-letter word.

Example

She spread the sweet HY on her toast.   <u>ONE</u>

1. The protesters were carrying PLADS. _____

2. She put the FERS into the tall vase. _____

3. All the cards were put into ENVEES and posted. _____

4. The staff had lunch in the TEEN. _____

5. The ancient HEDRAL was in the centre of the city. _____

6. It was a nasty injury, a torn LIGAT. _____

/6

Remove one letter from the word in capitals to leave a new word.
The meaning of the new word is given in the clue.

Example

WANT   an insect   <u>ANT</u>

   7. WAIVE   signal   _____

   8. QUILT   leave   _____

   9. TROUGH   uneven   _____

   10. PRIVET   nail or bolt   _____

   11. KNEEL   part of a ship _____

   12. ERASE   rest   _____

/6

Look carefully at the first two pairs of words.
Complete the third pair in the same way.

Example

cat, cart   ten, tern   ban, ?   <u>barn</u>

   13. cave, caver   dive, diver   live, _____

   14. broke, broken   woke, woken   spoke, _____

   15. dilute, dilution create, creation donate, _____

   16. pears, spear   pawns, spawn   pores, _____

   17. big, bag   rig, rag   wig, _____

   18. whole, hole   when, hen   what, _____

/6

Look carefully at these letter sequences. Work out the patterns to find the next letters in each sequence. The alphabet is here to help you.

A B C D E F G H I J K L M N O P Q R S T U V W X Y Z

Example

AB   DE   GH   JK   ?   <u>MN</u>

19. ML   NO   KJ   PQ   IH   _____

20. AE   BF   CG   DH   _____

21. ZA   YB   XC   WD   _____

22. EC   JH   OM   TR   _____

23. DH   GK   JN   MQ   _____

24. YX   WU   TS   RP   ON   _____

/6

Which of the following words **cannot** be made from the letters of the word in capitals? Underline the word.

Example

STATIONERY   state   stone   <u>towns</u>   notes   train

25. GERANIUM   grain   merge   germ   mare   near

26. TRIBAL   rib   rail   ball   bait   rat

27. OLYMPICS   mops   sly   limp   pole   slim

28. METALLIC   meal   tale   leant   melt   calm

29. HELICOPTER   rope   path   three   clip   price

30. HOPEFUL   hope   full   lope   fuel   flop

/6

Write these words into the grid so that they can be read across and down the grid.

Example

TOP   TIN   NAY   PAY

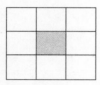

31. NOW   PIN   DEW   PAD

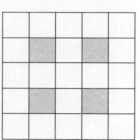

32. DUSTY
EARLY
PACED
PASTE
SITES
CATER

/2

Rearrange the capital letters to form a correctly spelt word that will complete these sentences sensibly. Write the word on the answer line.

Example

She led the horse to the ABTESL.   STABLE

33. The ERAGAG phoned to say that the car was ready. _____

34. It was NGROUPI with rain. _____

35. They lit the DCLAEN silently. _____

36. The peacock was preening its THRSEEAF. _____

37. The CKMOHMA was slung between two palm trees. _____

38. She loved browsing through the books in the RAYLIRB. _____

/6

Choose two words, one from each set of brackets, so that the second pair of words is completed in the same way as the first pair. Underline the words.

Example

Cow is to (milk, <u>calf,</u> herd) as horse is to (jump, saddle, <u>foal</u>).

39. Foot is to (toes, shoe, leg) as hand is to (hold, glove, ring).

40. Grass is to (hay, mower, green) as rose is to (perfume, red, love).

41. Sail is to (wind, balloon, yacht) as propeller is to (noise, metal, helicopter).

42. Rhubarb is to (stalk, crumble, sugar) as cabbage is to (caterpillar, leaf, dinner).

43. Sand is to (castle, beach, holiday) as ice is to (glacier, cold, winter).

44. Smile is to (happy, grin, face) as tear is to (old, sad, handkerchief).

/6

Move one letter from the first word and add it to the second word, to make two new, correctly spelt words. The order of the letters **cannot** be changed.

Example

plain   pad   →   <u>plan</u>   <u>paid</u>

45. crater   ban   →   _____   _____

46. waiter   pan   →   _____   _____

47. blender   rush   →   _____   _____

48. portion   wing   →   _____   _____

49. string   band   →   _____   _____

50. simile   con   →   _____   _____

/6

/50

PAPER 9

Choose two words, one from each set of brackets, so that the second pair of words is completed in the same way as the first pair. Underline the words.

Example

Cow is to (milk, <u>calf</u>, herd) as horse is to (jump, saddle, <u>foal</u>).

1. Cow is to (hay, milk, fresian) as hen is to (farmyard, cockerel, egg).

2. Microscope is to (scientist, sight, cells) as microphone is to (speaker, music, sound).

3. Apple is to (pie, crunchy, fruit) as spinach is to (healthy, muscle, vegetable).

4. Chalk is to (blackboard, mineral, granite) as meat is to (bread, chops, animal).

5. People are to (patients, surgery, doctors) as animals are to (cases, pets, vets).

6. Flock is to (shepherd, sheep, crowd) as gaggle is to (giggles, laughter, geese).

/6

In each of these sentences below, there is a four-letter word hidden across two words. The letters are in the right order and make a correctly spelt word. Write the word.

Example

It was fi<u>sh and</u> chips for supper.   <u>hand</u>

7. It was coffee time. _____

8. He was so hungry, he ate the whole thing! _____

9. Everyone ate apple pie at the harvest supper. _____

10. Your surprise visit hindered the proceedings. _____

11. The horses were all ready to go. _____

12. The vote was carried unanimously. _____

/6

Rearrange the capital letters to form a correctly spelt word that will complete these sentences sensibly. Write the word on the answer line.

Example

She led the horse to the ABTESL.   STABLE

13. There was a beautiful UNOAFITN in the middle of the garden. _____

14. There was great excitement when the RCIUCS came to town. _____

15. The birthday party was on USRAYATD. _____

16. Smoke was belching out of the HIMENCY. _____

17. On holiday they had ASETAKBRF by the beach. _____

18. The washing NEACHIM started to leak. _____

/6

Write these words into the grid so that they can be read across and down the grid.

Example

TOP   TIN   NAY   PAY

T	O	P
I		A
N	A	Y

19. COB   PIT   BAT   CUP

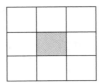

20. RISEN
HERON
MOTOR
REEDS
MARCH
THEIR

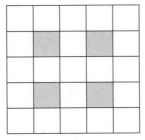

/2

In each group of five words, there are three words that go together in some way. Identify the two words that **do not** belong to the group and underline them.

Example

cat   <u>cockerel</u>   donkey   camel   <u>python</u>

21. triangle   circle   sphere   square   cylinder

22. mint   rosemary   vinegar   thyme   cloves

23. saw   bucket   hammer   secateurs   scythe

24. handbag   sandal   trainer   scarf   boot

25. Asteroid   Venus   Saturn   Mars   Satellite

26. liver   finger   heart   brain   arm

/6

In each sentence below, the word in capitals has three letters missing. The missing letters make a proper three-letter word on their own. Write the three-letter word.

Example

She spread the sweet HY on her toast.   <u>ONE</u>

27. The boys found sums with FRIONS very hard to do. _____

28. They couldn't wait for the summer HOAY! _____

29. The old lady was delighted to receive a TER. _____

30. They had gooseberry crumble and CUSD for pudding. _____

31. She loved watching the MONS swinging from tree to tree. _____

32. The visitors were entertained by a string QUET. _____

/6

Substitute the values for the letters and work out these equations. Give the answers as a letter.

Example

If A = 2, B = 5, C = 8, D = 12 and E = 20, what is the value of A × E ÷ C = ?   B̲

If A = 24, B = 2, C = 12, D = 8 and E = 6, what is the value of:

33. A ÷ D × B = _____

34. D − E × C = _____

35. B × C + A ÷ E = _____

If A = 2, B = 3, C = 15, D = 10 and E = 20, what is the value of:

36. A + B + C = _____

37. D + E ÷ A = _____

38. C × A ÷ B = _____

/6

Look carefully at the given codes and work out the answers to the questions.

Example

If the code for STEAM is 32415, what does the code 341 stand for?   S̲E̲A̲

If the code for CONTENT is 1234534:

39. What is the code for CONE? _____

40. What does the code 3245 stand for? _____

41. What is the code for COT? _____

If the codes for PIN, DIP and PEN are 245, 342 and 215:

42. What is the code for NIP? _____

43. What does the code 3451 stand for? _____

44. What is the code for PIE? _____

/6

Look carefully at the first two pairs of words, and then complete the third pair in the same way.

Example

cat, cart   ten, tern   ban, ?   _barn_

45. mad, moon   bad, boon   sad, _____

46. wild, will   child, chill   mild, _____

47. popper, pop   fatter, fat   robber, _____

48. sky, skies   cry, cries   fly, _____

49. bringing, big   ringing, rig   flinging, _____

50. bead, bad   dead, dad   head, _____

/6

/50

PAPER 10

Remove one letter from the word in capitals to leave a new word. The meaning of the new word is given in the clue.

Example

WANT   an insect   _ANT_

1. FLAVOUR   kindness   _____

2. CRAMP   site   _____

3. FRIEND   brute   _____

4. FEATHER   parent   _____

5. STRING   smart   _____

6. BUNGLE   instrument   _____

/6

Which of the following words **cannot** be made from the letters of the word in capitals? Underline the word.

Example

STATIONERY   state   stone   <u>towns</u>   notes   train

7. CANCEL   cane   lane   clan   cell   lance

8. CAMERA   came   care   calm   ream   race

9. KITCHEN   kite   tick   neck   chick   hint

10. CERTAINLY   carton   train   clay   tiny   lace

11. CHARMING   caring   harm   night   inch   grain

12. FELINE   fine   line   fen   feel   fell

/6

Look carefully at the given codes and work out the answers to the questions.

Example

If the code for STEAM is 32415, what does the code 341 stand for?   <u>SEA</u>

If the code for THEATRE is 3124352:

13. What is the code for HARE? _____

14. What does the code 35243 stand for? _____

15. What is the code for EARTH? _____

If the codes for COW, CON and NEW are 453, 124 and 123, but not in that order:

16. What is the code for WON? _____

17. What does the code 4524 stand for? _____

/6

18. What is the code for ONCE? _____

Move one letter from the first word and add it to the second word to make two new, correctly spelt words. The order of the letters **cannot** be changed.

Example

plain   pad → <u>plan</u>   <u>paid</u>

19. bean   kit → _____   _____

20. spend   hoe → _____   _____

21. wield   nigh → _____   _____

22. core   rash → _____   _____

23. wind   dine → _____   _____

24. trifle   able → _____   _____

/6

In each of these sentences below, there is a four-letter word hidden across two words. The letters are in the right order and make a correctly spelt word. Write the word.

Example

It was fi<u>sh and</u> chips for supper.   <u>hand</u>

25. Madam asked to see you tomorrow. _____

26. Did you watch the game yesterday? _____

27. The terrific art exhibition went around the country. _____

28. Were you there when the debate started? _____

29. The horses jumped over the gate. _____

/6

30. Half our time will be spent with the other club. _____

Answer booklet: Verbal Reasoning
Page 9–10

Paper 1
1. Monday — Summer
2. hedgehog — fox
3. strawberry — straw
4. mirror — magnet
5. turbulent — chaotic
6. slow — minute
7. OUR   8. AIR
9. PUT   10. DEN
11. TIN   12. OAR
13. dare   14. slimmer
15. fail   16. bind
17. char   18. pane

Answers may vary:

19.

C	A	R
U		O
T	U	B

20.

F	O	G
E		U
N	O	T

21. saucer, fork
22. late, evening
23. white, green
24. arm, neck
25. farming, gardening
26. cold, short
27. sting, crash
28. bad, feed
29. ring, down
30. read, blend
31. bat, meat/mate
32. bolder, cloud
33. D   34. B   35. B
36. E   37. A   38. B
39. treat   40. colt
41. drips   42. fried
43. sauna   44. equate
45. OLDER   46. BUSHES
47. METAL   48. PATENT
49. WELD   50. RANCH

Paper 2
1. triangle — circle
2. sticky — gluey
3. orchestra — quartet
4. miser — pauper
5. gold — silver
6. marzipan — sultana
7. MO   8. JH   9. IL
10. JI   11. ET   12. VU
13. D   14. A   15. A
16. C   17. E   18. C
19. HOLIDAYS 20. KITCHEN
21. BEAUTIFUL 22. GATEAU
23. BANDAGE 24. TRUMPET
25. TEAR   26. 4251
27. PEAR   28. 2145
29. PENCE   30. 4554

Answers may vary:

31.

T	A	P
R		U
Y	A	P

32.

S	I	T
E		E
A	Y	E

33. range, ground
34. beak, crash
35. why, weed
36. lump, player
37. fog, brush
38. son, boat
39. tell   40. stop
41. feet   42. tear
43. soft   44. heal
45. COST   46. CENT
47. IRATE   48. BREATH
49. BANK   50. TILE

Paper 3
1. DEER   2. 241
3. RENT   4. 21463
5. NEST   6. 23623
7. COD   8. FAN
9. PAN   10. ARK
11. HUT   12. PET
13. doom   14. bite
15. trap   16. pair
17. fender   18. rack
19. EV   20. RT   21. IG
22. TJ   23. QP   24. IE
25. toad   26. still
27. pear   28. barrel
29. peace   30. ranch

Answers may vary:

31.

W	I	N
I		E
T	O	W

32.

L	I	T
A		I
P	O	P

33. square, cube
34. cub, kitten
35. feathers, scales
36. distance, mass
37. brush, pen
38. sweet, sour

There may be more than one word in some sentences:

39. star   40. love
41. rage   42. real
43. wash   44. down
45. PANCAKES
46. CINEMA
47. JOURNEY
48. ANIMALS
49. BLIZZARD
50. GREENHOUSE

Paper 4
Answers may vary:

1.

M	A	T
O		E
P	I	N

2.

D	A	B
A		U
Y	E	S

3. dusty, frosty
4. mansion, cottage
5. toffee, treacle
6. valley, dale
7. plate, saucer
8. ewe, mare
9. flake, drop
10. loaf, bunch
11. blue, red
12. author, composer
13. singing, reading
14. dark, dry
15. bear   16. meal
17. melt   18. rope
19. vest   20. done
21. ROCKERY 22. LEDGES
23. EVOLVE 24. ITCH
25. LINER 26. PLACE
27. E   28. C   29. C
30. D   31. A   32. A
33. war, palm 34. fill, drip
35. mist, open
36. camp, spies/scam, pipes
37. fatter, plot 38. read, branch
39. SR   40. RE   41. FH
42. JI   43. TY   44. BS
45. rotor   46. green
47. garage   48. tenet
49. squid   50. stone

Paper 5
1. path — track
2. tins — compost
3. programme — poster
4. competition — sell
5. cheap — bargain
6. carry — give
7. 4132   8. TREAT
9. 21435   10. 4265
11. BEAT   12. 5246
13. stain — trip
14. hopper — when
15. mile — spans
16. rate — grim
17. bush — plod
18. plan — want
19. pal   20. deal
21. sons   22. same
23. hear   24. waned

1

25. WX   26. KM   27. ES
28. GF   29. XV   30. HN

Answers may vary:

31.
T	A	B
U		A
B	O	A

32.
M	U	G
A		E
	N	E	T

33. NET   34. RUM
35. MEN   36. RAP
37. RAN   38. CAN
39. CANCEL   40. COUNTY
41. ANGER   42. PEAL
43. INCH   44. TINT
45. TOBOGGAN
46. CHILDREN
47. CINEMA
48. AMUSEMENT
49. ANNIVERSARY
50. EXHIBITION

Paper 6

1. 3144   2. TREE
3. 3125   4. 534
5. SAT   6. 42512
7. fast, narrow
8. bed, chair
9. fork, pepper
10. shoe, tie
11. deep, low
12. descend, fall

There may be more than one word in some sentences:

13. tear   14. hens
15. rent   16. seal
17. self   18. dove
19. dry   20. crow
21. tilt   22. ace
23. bind   24. rather
25. groan   26. tell
27. view   28. apple
29. tenth   30. trite

Answers may vary:

31.
F	A	D
I		A
B	U	Y

32.
W	I	T
A		O
S	A	W

33. HIT   34. CAN
35. PUT   36. MEN
37. WIN   38. KIN
39. E   40. B   41. D
42. D   43. E   44. D
45. MEADOW   46. LIMOUSINE
47. FACTORY   48. MEMORIES
49. WEALTHY   50. CERTIFICATES

Paper 7

1. summer, autumn
2. hospital, office
3. skirt, trousers
4. blinds, curtains
5. historical, fictional
6. snap, swimming
7. 241   8. TAP

9. 4123   10. 542
11. SET   12. 3541
13. wind   pine
14. furry   flame
15. lumber   tramp
16. cot   stones
17. beak   prawn
18. founder   seal

There may be more than one word in some sentences:

19. full   20. near   21. shop
22. pint   23. talk   24. cane
25. TAR   26. PIT   27. LET
28. AIL   29. RIP   30. ICE
31. EH   32. PO   33. NF
34. RT   35. CP   36. RS
37. E   38. A   39. C
40. C   41. A   42. E

Answers may vary:

43.
R	O	D
U		A
M	U	D

44.
V	E	T
A		O
N	O	T

45. club   46. relate
47. lead   48. stir
49. flesh   50. actor

Paper 8

1. CAR   2. LOW
3. LOP   4. CAN
5. CAT   6. MEN
7. WAVE   8. QUIT
9. ROUGH   10. RIVET
11. KEEL   12. EASE
13. liver   14. spoken
15. donation   16. spore
17. wag   18. hat
19. RS   20. EI   21. VE
22. YW   23. PT   24. MK
25. merge   26. ball
27. pole   28. leant
29. path   30. full

Answers may vary:

31.
P	I	N
A		O
D	E	W

32.
P	A	C	E	D
A		A		U
S	I	T	E	S
T		E		T
E	A	R	L	Y

33. GARAGE   34. POURING
35. CANDLE   36. FEATHERS
37. HAMMOCK   38. LIBRARY
39. shoe, glove   40. green, red
41. yacht, helicopter
42. stalk, leaf
43. beach, glacier
44. happy, sad
45. cater/crate   barn/bran
46. water   pain
47. lender   brush
48. potion   wring
49. sting   brand
50. smile   coin/icon

Paper 9

1. milk, egg
2. sight, sound
3. fruit, vegetable
4. mineral, animal
5. doctors, vets
6. sheep, geese

There may be more than one word in some sentences:

7. feet   8. heat   9. neat
10. thin   11. real   12. scar
13. FOUNTAIN
14. CIRCUS
15. SATURDAY
16. CHIMNEY
17. BREAKFAST
18. MACHINE

Answers may vary:

19.
C	U	P
O		I
B	A	T

20.
M	A	R	C	H
O		E		E
T	H	E	I	R
O		D		O
R	I	S	E	N

21. sphere, cylinder
22. vinegar, cloves
23. bucket, hammer
24. handbag, scarf
25. Asteroid, Satellite
26. finger, arm
27. ACT   28. LID
29. LET   30. TAR
31. KEY   32. ART
33. E   34. A   35. D
36. E   37. C   38. D
39. 1235   40. NOTE
41. 124   42. 542
43. DINE   44. 241
45. soon   46. mill
47. rob   48. flies
49. fig   50. had

Paper 10

1. FAVOUR   2. CAMP
3. FIEND   4. FATHER
5. STING   6. BUGLE
7. cell   8. calm
9. chick   10. carton
11. night   12. fell
13. 1452   14. TREAT
15. 24531   16. 324
17. NEON   18. 2415
19. ban   kite
20. send   hope
21. wild   neigh
22. ore   crash
23. win   dined
24. rifle   table
25. mask   26. eyes
27. cart   28. test
29. dove   30. four
31. JK   32. RT   33. EV
34. SM   35. IJ   36. QE

37. C 38. D 39. E
40. B 41. D 42. A
Answers may vary:

43.
W	I	T
O		I
W	A	N

44.
P	A	P	E	R
A		O		E
N	O	I	S	E
E		S		D
S	L	E	D	S

45. chestnut beige
46. mitten skirt
47. hedgehog lion
48. paragraph preface
49. chips fingers
50. attentive distracting

Paper 11
Answers may vary:

1.
K	I	T
I		O
N	O	W

2.
B	O	W
A	R	E
R	E	D

3. drink, food
4. piano, guitar
5. nail, wood
6. sewing, knitting
7. castle, garden
8. Judy, princess
9. train sticks
10. fog brook
11. mash fritter
12. tripe flinch
13. read stilt
14. bead bred
15. ASH 16. PIN 17. ARM
18. ROW 19. TEN 20. KEY
21. CLAM 22. TRADE
23. PLACE 24. OUNCE
25. CEASE 26. PATH
27. hear 28. pond 29. spin
30. tall 31. fee 32. done
33. E 34. E 35. D
36. A 37. C 38. C
39. MARATHON
40. CLIMBING
41. THEATRE 42. PRACTISE
43. ANIMALS 44. ALPHABET
45. dented 46. tract 47. eye
48. trump 49. green 50. ounce

Paper 12
1. train bicycle
2. turnip leek
3. cold hurricane
4. tambourine totem
5. student pupil
6. scarce meagre
7. USE 8. WIN
9. OFF 10. RAT
11. PEN 12. AND
13. tear 14. soft
15. dare 16. melt
17. fare 18. chin

19. dull 20. amen 21. take
22. mine 23. bed 24. dine
25. IT 26. TS 27. NM
28. XO 29. EI 30. EV
31. COCKEREL
32. AEROPLANE
33. MOUNTAINS
34. SHAWL
35. SAPLINGS 36. DRAGONFLY
37. 4253 38. TAME
39. 5324 40. 453
41. TAP 42. 2345
43. heavy, uneven
44. light, narrow
45. smile, tear 46. pupil, teacher
47. shoes, shirt
48. sultanas, prunes
Answers may vary:

49.
C	O	D
A		I
N	A	P

50.
B	E	D
A	Y	E
T	E	N

Paper 13
1. mouse rabbit
2. knife plate
3. dust carpet
4. iceberg lake
5. rocket satellite
6. field dam
7. AND 8. PEN 9. ORE
10. AMP 11. LEG 12. ROB
13. BRAN 14. TREAD
15. CATER 16. ANTHER
17. PUMP 18. FLAT
19. bend 20. cape
21. mower 22. keel
23. panic 24. car
25. E 26. B 27. C
28. B 29. E 30. D
31. leaper 32. tent
33. carter 34. racer
35. firing 36. noon
Answers may vary:

37.
W	A	D
O		E
N	U	N

38.
B	O	O
A	D	D
R	E	D

39. 5214 40. TEE
41. 3143 42. 3145
43. STEW 44. 56451
45. HQ 46. MO 47. FG
48. DQ 49. QR 50. HB

Paper 14
1. ogre, giant
2. concerto, drums
3. stamp, delivery
4. storm, blizzard
5. plastic, paper
6. helicopter, jet
7. 5124 8. PALE
9. 54113 10. 1243

11. FEAR 12. 6243
13. beach prick
14. fame kilt
15. manger coat
16. trivia lover
17. petty crow
18. seep where
Answers may vary:

19.
R	O	B
A		O
T	A	X

20.
R	A	T	E	S
I		I		I
P	O	L	A	R
E		E		E
R	I	S	E	N

21. wand 22. text
23. west 24. play
25. lent 26. grow
27. TROUGH 28. MENTAL
29. GRIME 30. PRICE
31. WAITER 32. SHIFT
33. WO 34. KL 35. NL
36. QE 37. HT 38. BW
39. WATCH 40. ORCHARD
41. FAIRIES 42. FLOWERS
43. PICTURE 44. APRICOTS
45. level 46. steer
47. thistle 48. cook
49. spit 50. three

Paper 15
Answers may vary:

1.
S	O	B
A		A
T	E	A

2.
P	O	P
A	N	A
L	E	T

3. beef, mutton
4. yolk, ruby
5. teapot, mug
6. poetry, dictionary
7. shorts, trousers
8. slice, pack
9. coal, biscuits
10. lake, river
11. black, blunt
12. foolish, young
13. emerald, sapphire
14. claw, beak
There may be more than one word in some sentences:
15. move 16. punt 17. twin
18. grub 19. wasp 20. hand
21. ban 22. mall 23. cap
24. frame 25. road 26. cattle
27. QR 28. ED 29. FJ
30. AW 31. SU 32. YA
33. eye 34. tree 35. race
36. chain 37. realm 38. dia
39. mat spines
40. chin acorn
41. rice carp
42. lead spoon
43. fried sand
44. paced plump

Paper 16
1. cash, wallet
2. panda, elephant
3. cheese, salad
4. lighthouse, planetarium
5. starfish, urchin
6. desk, table
7. tart/star   8. keel
9. wind   10. glad
11. them   12. chap
13. PUPPET   14. CROCODILE
15. TICKET   16. CERTAIN
17. SUDDENLY 18. BAMBOO
19. KIPPER   20. LODGE
21. CARTED   22. FASTED
23. RIFLE   24. TOUGH
Answers may vary:

25.

P	A	L
U		I
T	O	P

26.

B	A	S	T	E
I		A		V
T	I	T	L	E
E		I		R
S	U	N	N	Y

27. 3142   28. VAN
29. 2425   30. 545
31. SHOP   32. 341
33. marmalade, cheese
34. bite, sting
35. lower, descend
36. eyes, ears
37. hand, foot
38. horse, hen
39. JAM   40. TRY
41. ALL   42. RAP
43. THE   44. ORE
45. beautiful   46. man
47. meat   48. wand
49. sane   50. into

Paper 17
Answers may vary:

1.

D	O	T
A		A
M	I	X

2.

P	A	S	T	E
A		C		A
D	R	E	A	R
R		N		L
E	N	T	R	Y

3. flavour, scent
   dollar, pound
   second, first
   onds, clubs
     temperature
      al
         OUR   11. RAM
         RAN   14. EAT
       ore than one word
     s:
     4   sofa

---

17. only   18. mean
19. tour   20. chin
21. SORT   22. AFTER
23. FOUNDER 24. SIGHT
25. COMPOSE 26. COMA
27. RUCKSACK 28. LANTERN
29. POSITIVE 30. CAMERA
31. LESSONS 32. VOLCANO
33. trip   beat
34. flan   knit
35. each   bale
36. camper   slice
37. nail   cast
38. gas   panthers
39. wine   40. singer
41. cop   42. slow
43. mug   44. bats
45. E   46. E   47. D
48. B   49. E   50. E

Paper 18
1. HI   2. SP   3. EC
4. DB   5. VQ   6. OT
7. A   8. A   9. B
10. C   11. A   12. C
13. spine   14. place
15. riper   16. treat
17. cereal   18. wish
Answers may vary:

19.

S	A	D
U		I
M	A	P

20.

B	O	A
E	A	T
E	R	E

21. moth   spider
22. alone   solitary
23. beak   claw
24. clay   silt
25. stamp   boots
26. pan   dish
27. 3461
28. MEAL
29. 2543
30. 1342
31. PIP
32. 524421
33. fright   care
34. stop   camp
35. feet   blest
36. swig   dines
37. caters/crates   brought
38. flit   bang
39. TOP
40. ASK
41. SHE
42. RUN
43. PEA
44. KIN
45. SWINE
46. BLOCKED

---

47. COUNTRY
48. CRAMPED
49. SHALLOW
50. SEDGE

Paper 19
1. 3451
2. PEAT
3. 4213
4. 2345
5. NIT
6. 2153
7. butter, cherry
8. ladle, carve
9. trumpet, lighthouse
10. fabric, leather
11. computer, library
12. time, distance
13. ANGLE
14. AMBER
15. DIRECTOR
16. ENVY
17. FINAL
18. GILT
Answers may vary:

19.

C	A	B
O	D	E
O	D	D

20.

W	I	G
A	C	E
N	E	T

21. ROT
22. ARM
23. CAT
24. AND
25. PIT
26. CUP
27. wine   chore
28. shed   port
29. action   raft
30. raised   wasp
31. lock   flap
32. smile   rain
33. QG
34. FE
35. EH
36. HQ
37. ZE
38. CK
39. HAMSTER
40. FOSSILS
41. MANUSCRIPT
42. POSITIONS
43. DIVED
44. GALAXY
45. longer
46. meet
47. gong
48. amiss
49. strain
50. sunny

Look carefully at these letter sequences. Work out the patterns to find the next letters in each sequence. The alphabet is here to help you.

A B C D E F G H I J K L M N O P Q R S T U V W X Y Z

Example

AB   DE   GH   JK   ?   <u>MN</u>

31. RS   PQ   NO   LM   _____

32. FH   IK   LN   OQ   _____

33. AN   BP   CR   DT   _____

34. WQ   VP   UO   TN   _____

35. AB   DC   EF   HG   _____

36. YA   WB   UC   SD   _____

/6

Substitute the values for the letters and work out these equations. Give each answer as a letter.

Example

If A = 2, B = 5, C = 8, D = 12 and E = 20, what is the value of A × E ÷ C = ?   <u>B</u>

If A = 2, B = 5, C = 8, D = 16 and E = 24, what is the value of:

37. E − C ÷ A = _____

38. B × C − E = _____

39. E + D + C ÷ A = _____

If A = 3, B = 7, C = 12, D = 21 and E = 2, what is the value of:

40. A × B − E − C = _____

41. C + B + E = _____

42. C × E − D = _____

Write these words into the grid so that they can be read across and down the grid.

Example

TOP   TIN   NAY   PAY

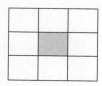

43. WIT   WAN   TIN   WOW

44. PAPER
NOISE
REEDS
PANES
SLEDS
POISE

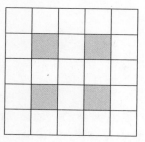

/2

In each group of five words, there are three words that go together in some way. Identify the two words that **do not** belong to the group and underline them.

Example

cat   <u>cockerel</u>   donkey   camel   <u>python</u>

45. magenta   chestnut   crimson   red   beige

46. mitten   bonnet   cap   skirt   beret

ox   hedgehog   cow   buffalo   lion

ctive   noun   paragraph   preface   verb

/6

e   chips   cod   fingers   haddock

48   attentive   astonishing   remarkable   distracting

/50

PAPER 11

Write these words into the grid so that they can be read across and down the grid.

Example

TOP   TIN   NAY   PAY

T	O	P
I		A
N	A	Y

1. KIT   NOW   KIN   TOW

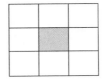

2. BOW   RED   ARE   WED   ORE   BAR

/2

Choose two words, one from each set of brackets, so that the second pair of words is completed in the same way as the first pair. Underline the words.

Example

Cow is to (milk, calf, herd) as horse is to (jump, saddle, foal).

3. Tea is to (cup, drink, teapot) as cake is to (birthday, knife, food).

4. Keys are to (piano, tune, sonata) as strings are to (chords, strumming, guitar).

5. Hammer is to (screw, coal, nail) as saw is to (cutting, sawdust, wood).

6. Thread is to (sewing, needle, patchwork) as wool is to (jumper, knitting, kitten).

7. Moat is to (hillock, castle, courtyard) as wall is to (stones, garden, gate).

8. Punch is to (holiday, show, Judy) as prince is to (fairy, princess, maiden).

/6

Move one letter from the first word and add it to the second word, to make two new, correctly spelt words. The order of the letters **cannot** be changed.

Example

plain   pad → <u>plan</u>   <u>paid</u>

9. strain   ticks → _____ _____

10. frog   book → _____ _____

11. marsh   fitter → _____ _____

12. triple   finch → _____ _____

13. tread   silt → _____ _____

14. bread   bed → _____ _____

/6

In each sentence below, the word in capitals has three letters missing. The missing letters make a proper three-letter word on their own. Write the three-letter word.

Example

She spread the sweet HY on her toast.   <u>ONE</u>

15. The clean WING was hung out on the line. _____

16. They enjoyed SHOPG in the new mall. _____

He had toast and MALADE every morning. _____

children were delighted to see the Queen's CN. _____

re is no music, we will have to PRED! _____

50 really looking forward to her first game of HOC. _____

/6

Remove one letter from the word in capitals to leave a new word. The meaning of the new word is given in the clue.

Example

WANT   an insect   <u>ANT</u>

21. CLAIM   shellfish   _____

22. TIRADE   buying and selling   _____

23. PLAICE   location   _____

24. POUNCE   weight   _____

25. CREASE   stop   _____

26. PATCH   footway   _____

/6

Look carefully at the first two pairs of words, and then complete the third pair in the same way.

Example

cat, cart   ten, tern   ban, ?   <u>barn</u>

27. den, dean   led, lead   her, _____

28. found, fond   bound, bond   pound, _____

29. pun, spun   tone, stone   pin, _____

30. walk, wall   milk, mill   talk, _____

31. weep, wee   teen, tee   feed, _____

32. cons, cone   tons, tone   dons, _____

/6

Substitute the values for the letters and work out these equations. Give each answer as a letter.

Example

If $A = 2$, $B = 5$, $C = 8$, $D = 12$ and $E = 20$, what is the value of $A \times E \div C = ?$ <u>B</u>

If $A = 10$, $B = 2$, $C = 3$, $D = 14$ and $E = 20$, what is the value of:

33. $B \times C + D =$ _____

34. $D \div B + A + C =$ _____

35. $E - A - C \times B =$ _____

If A = 8, B = 4, C = 16, D = 2 and E = 24, what is the value of:

36. C ÷ B × D = _____

37. E ÷ B + A + D = _____

38. A × B − C = _____   /6

Rearrange the capital letters to form a correctly spelt word that
will complete these sentences sensibly. Write the word on the
answer line.

Example

She led the horse to the ABTESL.   STABLE

39. They trained for weeks before running the RAMANTOH. _____

40. Once attached to the ropes, they began GCNIMLBI the steep cliff. _____

41. Her favourite play was being performed in the new ETETHAR. _____

42. He used to SEACPRTI every day. _____

43. The children loved being able to touch the IALMNAS at the farm. _____

44. The ELABTPAH was printed around the edge of the classroom. _____   /6

Which of the following words **cannot** be made from the letters of
the word in capitals? Underline the word.

Example

STATIONERY   state   stone   towns   notes   train

45. ANIMATED   made   named   timed   dented   denim

46. CARTOON   cart   torn   tract   croon   carton

47. BAKERY   beak   rake   bye   bray   eye

48. PERIMETER   prime   metre   trump   riper   tripe

49. GLE   glen   green   grain   great   tingle   /6

52 ICY   cure   cry   ounce   rye   curry   /50

PAPER 12

In each group of five words below, there are three words that go together in some way. Identify the two words that **do not** belong to the group and underline them.

Example

cat   <u>cockerel</u>   donkey   camel   <u>python</u>

1. van   lorry   train   bicycle   car

2. plum   turnip   cherry   apple   leek

3. northerly   cold   westerly   hurricane   easterly

4. tripod   tambourine   triple   triangle   totem

5. tutor   teacher   student   lecturer   pupil

6. plentiful   scarce   meagre   abundant   ample

/6

In each sentence below, the word in capitals has three letters missing. The missing letters make a proper three-letter word on their own. Write the three-letter word.

Example

She spread the sweet HY on her toast.   <u>ONE</u>

7. They had waterproof TRORS for the hike. _____

8. The TER days were dark and cold. _____

9. The friends all met up in town for CEE and a chat. _____

10. The surgeon scrubbed up before carrying out the OPEION. _____

11. The young CARTER did some intricate wood carvings. _____

12. At the fair, the children had CYFLOSS and went on the big dipper. _____

/6

In each of these sentences, there is a four-letter word hidden across two words. The letters are in the right order and make a correctly spelt word. Write the word.

Example

It was fi<u>sh and</u> chips for supper.   <u>hand</u>

13. The late arrival of the plane upset their plans. _____

14. The dogs often carried the slippers around the house. _____

15. The large grassed area was well kept. _____

16. Travelling by camel took the party two days. _____

17. The hat and scarf are from very fine wool. _____

18. He decided to branch into a new line of products. _____

/6

Look carefully at the first two pairs of words, and then complete the third pair in the same way.

Example

cat, cart   ten, tern   ban, ?   <u>barn</u>

19. bench, bunch   fen, fun   dell, _____

20. wake, awake   jar, ajar   men, _____

21. stones, tone   stripes, tripe   stakes, _____

22. fiddle, middle   found, mound   fine, _____

23. plant, pat   croon, con   bread, _____

24. wins, wine   fins, fine   dins, _____

/6

Look carefully at these letter sequences. Work out the patterns to find the next letters in each sequence. Write them on the answer line. The alphabet is here to help you.

A B C D E F G H I J K L M N O P Q R S T U V W X Y Z

Example

AB   DE   GH   JK   ?   <u>MN</u>

25. AP   CQ   ER   GS   _____

26. DC   HG   LK   PO   _____

27. ZY   WV   TS   QP   _____

28. TK   UL   VM   WN   _____

29. AE   BF   CG   DH   _____

30. AZ   BY   CX   DW   _____

/6

Rearrange the capital letters to form a correctly spelt word that will complete these sentences sensibly. Write the word on the answer line.

Example

She led the horse to the ABTESL.   <u>STABLE</u>

31. The crowing of the LOCCKEER woke them every morning. _____

32. The EPLOARNAE was full of holidaymakers. _____

33. The snow-capped NTAMINSOU were visible in the distance. _____

34. She pulled the warm HSWLA closely around her shoulders. _____

35. They planted a row of LINPGSSA to replace the old trees. _____

36. The blue DGYONFLRA was hovering over the pond. _____

/6

Look carefully at the given codes and work out the answers to the questions.

Example

If the code for STEAM is 32415, what does the code 341 stand for?   <u>SEA</u>

If the code for METAL is 53124:

37. What is the code for LAME? _____

38. What does the code 1253 stand for? _____

39. What is the code for MEAL? _____

If the codes for SEA, TEE and PAT are 134, 245 and 533, but not in that order:

40. What is the code for ATE? _____

41. What does the code 542 stand for? _____

42. What is the code for PEAT? _____

/6

Choose two words, one from each set of brackets, so that the second pair of words is completed in the same way as the first pair. Underline the words.

Example

Cow is to (milk, <u>calf,</u> herd) as horse is to (jump, saddle, <u>foal</u>).

43. Light is to (bulb, switch, heavy) as smooth is to (velvet, creamy, uneven).

44. Heavy is to (coal, weight, light) as wide is to (narrow, ribbon, broad).

45. Happy is to (laughing, smile, joy) as sad is to (fear, black, tear).

46. Learning is to (pupil, school, book) as teaching is to (lessons, class, teacher).

47. Laces are to (feet, shoes, knots) as buttons are to (buttonhole, sewing, shirt).

48. Grapes are to (sultanas, wine, vineyard) as plums are to (pudding, prunes, custard).

/6

Write these words into the grid so that they can be read across and down the grid.

Example

TOP   TIN   NAY   PAY

49. COD   NAP   CAN   DIP

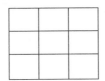

50. DEN   AYE   TEN   BAT   EYE   BED

/6

/50

PAPER 13

In each group of five words below, there are three words that go together in some way. Identify the two words that **do not** belong to the group and underline them.

Example

cat   <u>cockerel</u>   donkey   camel   <u>python</u>

1. mouse   buzzard   eagle   hawk   rabbit

2. butter   knife   jam   bread   plate

3.	flex	dust	plug	wire	carpet
4.	river	iceberg	lake	stream	brook
5.	star	moon	rocket	satellite	planet
6.	copse	forest	field	dam	wood

/6

In each sentence below, the word in capitals has three letters missing. The missing letters make a proper three-letter word on their own. Write the three-letter word.

Example

She spread the sweet HY on her toast.   <u>ONE</u>

7. He was very hungry so he ate the last SWICH. _____

8. The film showed the GUINS huddled together on the ice. _____

9. They cycled for miles along the tracks in the FST. _____

10. The boys were excited about the CING holiday. _____

11. The COLE students came back for the new term. _____

12. The children found the PLEM solving questions very hard. _____

/6

Remove one letter from the word in capitals to leave a new word. The meaning of the new word is given in the clue.

Example

WANT   an insect   <u>ANT</u>

13. BRAND   food for horses   _____

14. THREAD   · step   _____

15. CANTER   prepare food   _____

16. PANTHER   part of flower   _____

17. PLUMP   draw up water   _____

18. FLOAT   level   _____

/6

Look carefully at the first two pairs of words.
Complete the third pair in the same way.

Example

cat, cart   ten, tern   ban, ?   _barn_

19. plush, push   flour, four   blend, _____

20. scrap, scrape   trip, tripe   cap, _____

21. cow, cower   flow, flower   mow, _____

22. stop, pots   pool, loop   leek, _____

23. come, comic   state, static   pane, _____

24. potato, pot   petition, pet   carriage, _____

/6

Substitute the values for the letters and work out these
equations. Give each answer as a letter.

Example

If $A = 2$, $B = 5$, $C = 8$, $D = 12$ and $E = 20$, what is the value of $A \times E \div C = ?$ _B_

If $A = 10$, $B = 3$, $C = 5$, $D = 15$ and $E = 30$, what is the value of:

25. $B \times C + D =$ _____

26. $E - D \div C =$ _____

27. $A + E - D \div C =$ _____

If $A = 3$, $B = 8$, $C = 2$, $D = 18$ and $E = 4$, what is the value of:

28. $D \div A + C =$ _____

29. $D \times C \div A - B =$ _____

30. $A \times E + B - C =$ _____

/6

Which of the following words **cannot** be made from the letters of the word in capitals? Underline each word.

Example

STATIONERY   state   stone   <u>towns</u>   notes   train

31. REPLAY   leaper   pray   real   year   early

32. MENTION   mint   nine   tone   tent   time

33. TEACHER   chart   reach   ache   etch   carter

34. CAMERA   came   ream   racer   mace   cream

35. FOREIGN   fire   gone   ring   groin   firing

36. POSITION   post   spoon   sip   noon   pints

/6

Write these words into the grid so that they can be read across and down the grid.

Example

TOP   TIN   NAY   PAY

T	O	P
I		A
N	A	Y

37. DEN   NUN   WAD   WON

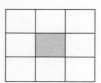

38. ODE   RED   BOO   BAR   ADD   ODD

/2

Look carefully at the given codes and work out the answers to the questions.

Example

If the code for STEAM is 32415, what does the code 341 stand for? <u>SEA</u>

If the code for REPEAT is 425213:

39. What is the code for PEAR? _____

40. What does the code 322 stand for? _____

41. What is the code for TART? _____

If the codes for SOW, WET and WAS are 364, 315 and 423, but not in that order:

42. What is the code for WEST? _____

43. What does the code 4513 stand for? _____

44. What is the code for TASTE? _____

/6

Look carefully at these letter sequences. Work out the patterns to find the next letters in each sequence. Write them on the answer line. The alphabet is here to help you.

A B C D E F G H I J K L M N O P Q R S T U V W X Y Z

Example

AB   DE   GH   JK   ?   <u>MN</u>

45. LM   KN   JO   IP   _____

46. AD   CE   FI   HJ   KN   _____

47. TU   WX   ZA   CD   _____

48. HM   NG   FO   PE   _____

/6

49. AB   FE   IJ   NM   _____

50. DX   EY   FZ   GA   _____

/50

PAPER 14

In each group of five words below, there are three words that go together in some way. Identify the two words that **do not** belong to the group and underline them.

Example

cat   <u>cockerel</u>   donkey   camel   <u>python</u>

1. pixie   ogre   gnome   elf   giant

2. choir   concerto   chorus   singing   drums

3. stamp   package   delivery   parcel   packet

4. danger   storm   hazard   peril   blizzard

5. gold   copper   plastic   paper   bronze

6. helicopter   catamaran   hovercraft   jet   yacht

/6

Look carefully at the given codes and work out the answers to the questions.

Example

If the code for STEAM is 32415, what does the code 341 stand for?   <u>SEA</u>

If the code for PLEASE is 341251:

7. What is the code for SEAL? _____

8. What does the code 3241 stand for? _____

9. What is the code for SLEEP? _____

If the codes for FIR, FEE and AFT are 124, 133 and 516, but not in that order:

10. What is the code for FIRE? _____

11. What does the code 1354 stand for? _____

12. What is the code for TIRE? _____

/6

Move one letter from the first word and add it to the second word, to make two new, correctly spelt words. The order of the letters cannot be changed.

Example

plain   pad   → <u>plan</u>   <u>paid</u>

13. breach   pick   → _____   _____

14. flame   kit   → _____   _____

15. manager   cot   → _____   _____

16. trivial   over   → _____   _____

17. pretty   cow   → _____   _____

18. sheep   were   → _____   _____

/6

Write these words into the grid so that they can be read across and down the grid.

Example

TOP   TIN   NAY   PAY

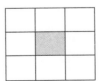

T	O	P
I		A
N	A	Y

19. BOX   TAX   RAT   ROB

20. SIREN
RATES
RIPER
TILES
POLAR
RISEN

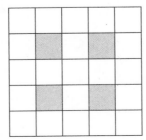

/2

63

In each of these sentences, there is a four-letter word hidden across two words. The letters are in the right order and make a correctly spelt word. Write the word.

Example

It was fi<u>sh and</u> chips for supper.   <u>hand</u>

21. Slow and steady wins the race. _____

22. They could set extra chairs round the large table. _____

23. Can you now estimate when you will arrive? _____

24. There was a deep layer of snow covering everything. _____

25. He was given a special entry ticket. _____

26. He loves running, rowing and cycling. _____

/6

Add one letter to the word in capitals to make a new word. The meaning of the new word is given in the clue.

Example

ANT   desire   <u>WANT</u>

27. ROUGH   water for horses   _____

28. METAL   state of mind   _____

29. GRIM   dirt   _____

30. RICE   cost   _____

31. WATER   server   _____

32. SIFT   change   _____

/6

Look carefully at these letter sequences. Work out the patterns to find the next letters in each sequence. Write them on the answer line. The alphabet is here to help you.

A B C D E F G H I J K L M N O P Q R S T U V W X Y Z

Example

AB   DE   GH   JK   ?   <u>MN</u>

33. AK   ZL   YM   XN   _____

34. BA   CD   FE   GH   JI   _____

35. ZX   VT   YW   US   RP   _____

36. MA   NB   OC   PD   _____

37. LP   KQ   JR   IS   _____

38. XS   YT   ZU   AV   _____

/6

Rearrange the capital letters to form a correctly spelt word that will complete these sentences sensibly. Write the word on the answer line.

Example

She led the horse to the ABTESL.   <u>STABLE</u>

39. She glanced at her CWTAH to check the time. _____

40. The sheep were grazing in the RCORHAD between the fruit trees. _____

41. The little girls loved to dress up as AIFEIRS. _____

42. The garden was a riot of colour with all the summer ORSFWEL. _____

43. He studies the REICPTU in great detail. _____

44. Some ROICPTAS are dried and others used for jam. _____

/6

Which of the following words **cannot** be made from the letters of the word in capitals? Underline the word.

Example

STATIONERY   state   stone   <u>towns</u>   notes   train

45. ENVELOPE   pole   love   even   level   noel

46. MATRESS   tram   stream   steer   steam   rest

47. WHISTLE   while   white   stile   thistle   wish

48. CROCKERY   rock   core   cook   rye   yore

49. PUPPETS   step   pup   pest   puts   spit

50. HEARTH   ear   heart   hear   three   rate

/6

/50

PAPER 15

Write these words into the grid so that they can be read across and down the grid.

Example

TOP   TIN   NAY   PAY

T	O	P
I		A
N	A	Y

1. SAT   TEA   SOB   BAA

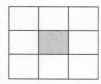

2. PAT   LET   ONE
    ANA   PAL   POP

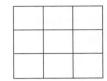

/2

In each group of five words below, there are three words that go together in some way. Identify the two words that **do not** belong to the group and underline them.

Example

cat   <u>cockerel</u>   donkey   camel   <u>python</u>

3. chicken   duck   goose   beef   mutton

4. milk   yolk   snow   frost   ruby

5. saucepan   wok   teapot   mug   frying-pan

6. novel   poetry   story   fiction   dictionary

7. dress   frock   pinafore   shorts   trousers

8. third   half   slice   pack   quarter

/6

Choose two words, one from each set of brackets, so that the second pair of words is completed in the same way as the first pair.

Example

Cow is to (milk, <u>calf</u>, herd) as horse is to (jump, saddle, <u>foal</u>).

9. Sack is to (paper, coal, race) as packet is to (biscuits, stamp, parcel).

10. Pond is to (duck, ice, lake) as stream is to (river, bridge, fish).

11. White is to (snow, black, crystal) as sharp is to (point, blunt, spike).

12. Wise is to (owl, ancient, foolish) as old is to (young, granny, slow).

13. Green is to (grass, emerald, leaf) as blue is to (paint, ink, sapphire).

14. Crab is to (lunch, claw, basket) as bird is to (beak, wing, eagle).

/6

In each of these sentences, there is a four-letter word hidden across two words. The letters are in the right order and make a correctly spelt word. Write the word.

Example

It was fi<u>sh and</u> chips for supper.   <u>hand</u>

15. The bees swarm over the hives in summer. _____

16. Let her sleep until morning. _____

17. May the best student win! _____

18. She removed the ring rubbing her finger. _____

19. It was, perhaps, the only time they would meet. _____

20. After the fourth and last performance, they went home. _____

/6

Look carefully at the first two pairs of words. Complete the third pair in the same way.

Example

cat, cart   ten, tern   ban, ?   <u>barn</u>

21. trip, tip   trap, tap   bran, _____

22. fellow, fall   bellow, ball   mellow, _____

23. west, wet   bent, bet   carp, _____

24. fight, fright   fitter, fritter   fame, _____

25. absent, sent   absolute, solute   abroad, _____

26. skit, skittle   net, nettle   cat, _____

/6

Look carefully at these letter sequences. Work out the patterns to find the next letters in each sequence. Write them on the answer line. The alphabet is here to help you.

A B C D E F G H I J K L M N O P Q R S T U V W X Y Z

Example

AB   DE   GH   JK   ?   <u>MN</u>

27. LK   MN   JI   OP   HG   _____

28. WV   TS   PO   KJ   _____

29. BF   CG   DH   EI   _____

30. EA   DZ   CY   BX   _____

31. CE   GI   KM   OQ   _____

32. CE   BD   AC   ZB   _____

/6

Which of the following words **cannot** be made from the letters of the word in capitals? Underline the word.

Example

STATIONERY   state   stone   <u>towns</u>   notes   train

33. JOURNEY   joy   our   urn   eye   run

34. ITINERANT   rant   near   tier   tent   tree

35. COURAGE   rage   racer   core   cure   grace

36. FANTASTIC   faint   chain   fast   scant   facts

37. MARKET   mark   realm   tram   tamer   take

38. SPLENDID   lend   lines   piled   dines   dials

/6

Move one letter from the first word and add it to the second word, to make two new, correctly spelt words. The order of the letters **cannot** be changed.

Example

plain   pad   →   <u>plan</u>   <u>paid</u>

39. mast   pines   →   _____   _____

40. chain   corn   →   _____   _____

41. price   car   →   _____   _____

42. plead   soon   →   _____   _____

43. friend   sad   →   _____   _____

44. placed   pump   →   _____   _____

/6

Substitute the values for the letters and work out these equations. Give each answer as a letter.

Example

If $A = 2$, $B = 5$, $C = 8$, $D = 12$ and $E = 20$, what is the value of $A \times E \div C = ?$ <u>B</u>

If $A = 3$, $B = 7$, $C = 1$, $D = 21$ and $E = 14$, what is the value of:

45. $D \div A + B =$ _____

46. $E \div B \times A + C =$ _____

47. $D + E \div B \times A - C =$ _____

If $A = 2$, $B = 5$, $C = 10$, $D = 15$ and $E = 40$, what is the value of:

48. $B \times C \div A \div B =$ _____

49. $C + B \times A - D =$ _____

50. $E \div B + A =$ _____

/6

/50

PAPER 16

In each group of five words below, there are three words that go together in some way. Identify the two words that **do not** belong to the group and underline them.

Example

cat   <u>cockerel</u>   donkey   camel   <u>python</u>

1. wage   cash   salary   pay   wallet

2. panda   seal   walrus   dolphin   elephant

3. roll   cheese   baguette   salad   loaf

4. lighthouse greenhouse orangery   conservatory   planetarium

5. winkle   mussel   starfish   urchin   limpet

6. desk   chair   stool   settee   table

/6

In each of these sentences there is a four-letter word hidden across two words. The letters are in the right order and make a correctly spelt word. Write the word.

Example

It was fi<u>sh and</u> chips for supper.   <u>hand</u>

7. He was the first artist to study abroad. _____

8. The giant sculptures make elephants look small! _____

9. They are taught to show individual samples to the visitors. _____

10. He was going laden with gifts. _____

11. They left after the meeting. _____

12. She checked each apple in turn. _____

/6

Rearrange the capital letters to form a correctly spelt word that will complete these sentences sensibly. Write the word on the answer line.

Example

She led the horse to the ABTESL. <u>STABLE</u>

13. The PUTEPP show kept them all entertained. _____

14. He jumped when the CILOCODRE snapped at a bird. _____

15. They had bought their return KEICTT the day before. _____

16. She was RCAINET she had put the money away safely. _____

17. LYDSDEUN there was a loud noise. _____

18. The delicate MOBABO shoots were just beginning to grow. _____

/6

Remove one letter from the word in capitals to leave a new word. The meaning of the new word is given in the clue.

Example

WANT   an insect   <u>ANT</u>

19. SKIPPER   fish   _____

20. LODGER   dwelling   _____

21. CHARTED   carried   _____

22. FEASTED   without food   _____

23. TRIFLE   gun   _____

24. THOUGH   hard   _____

/6

Write these words into the grid so that they can be read across and down the grid.

Example

TOP   TIN   NAY   PAY

T	O	P
I		A
N	A	Y

25. TOP   PAL   LIP   PUT

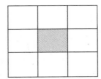

26. EVERY
BITES
SATIN
SUNNY
TITLE
BASTE

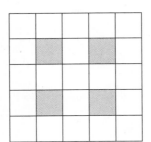

/2

Look carefully at the given codes and work out the answers to the questions.

Example

If the code for STEAM is 32415, what does the code 341 stand for?   <u>SEA</u>

If the code for HEAVEN is 321425:

27. What is the code for HAVE? _____

28. What does the code 415 stand for? _____

29. What is the code for EVEN? _____

If the codes for HIP, HOP and SIP are 345, 325 and 145, but not in that order:

30. What is the code for PIP? _____

31. What does the code 1325 stand for? _____

32. What is the code for HIS? _____

/6

Choose two words, one from each set of brackets, so that the second pair of words is completed in the same way as the first pair.

Example

Cow is to (milk, <u>calf,</u> herd) as horse is to (jump, saddle, <u>foal</u>).

33. Oranges are to (colour, breakfast, marmalade) as milk is to (cow, cheese, calcium).

34. Mosquito is to (midge, repellent, bite) as scorpion is to (tail, sting, danger).

35. Raise is to (lift, lower, hold) as ascend is to (descend, stairs, escalator).

36. Watch is to (time, wrist, eyes) as listen is to (music, ears, sound).

37. Thumb is to (grasp, hand, nail) as toe is to (sandals, foot, sole).

38. Stable is to (horse, saddle, reins) as coop is to (hen, eggs, corn).

/6

In each sentence below, the word in capitals has three letters missing. The missing letters make a proper three-letter word on their own. Write the three-letter word.

Example

She spread the sweet HY on her toast.   <u>ONE</u>

39. Her favourite PYAS matched her pink slippers. _____

40. The taxi set them down by the EN sign. _____

41. The foal was fathered by a famous STION. _____

42. The scientists plotted the results on a GH. _____

43. The WEAR forecast was very accurate this time. _____

44. Many EXPLRS have travelled along this route. _____

/6

Look carefully at the first two pairs of words, and then complete the third pair in the same way.

Example

cat, cart   ten, tern   ban, ?   <u>barn</u>

45. plenty, plentiful   bounty, bountiful   beauty, _____

46. forest, for   cottage, cot   mansion, _____

47. sweet, sweat   beet, beat   meet, _____

48. bandit, band   winded, wind   wander, _____

49. land, lane   wand, wane   sand, _____   /6

50. side, inside   put, input   to, _____

/50

PAPER 17

Write these words into the grid so that they can be read going across and down the grid.

Example

TOP   TIN   NAY   PAY

T	O	P
I		A
N	A	Y

1. DAM   MIX   TAX   DOT

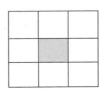

2. DREAR

EARLY

SCENT

PASTE

ENTRY

PADRE

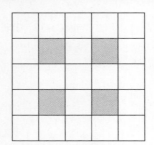

/2

> Choose two words, one from each set of brackets, so that the
> second pair of words is completed in the same way as the first pair.

Example

Cow is to (milk, <u>calf,</u> herd) as horse is to (jump, saddle, <u>foal</u>).

3. Taste is to (food, flavour, cooking) as smell is to (farm, sneeze, scent).

4. Cents is to (dollar, centimetres, coins) as pence is to (England, pound, copper).

5. Silver is to (cup, prize, second) as gold is to (watch, first, metal).

6. Hearts is to (cards, joker, diamonds) as spades is to (patience, clubs, black).

7. Scales is to (fish, weight, shop) as thermometer is to (temperature, doctor, ill).

8. Ewe is to (ram, spring, lamb) as mare is to (calf, foal, young).

/6

> In each sentence below, the word in capitals has three letters
> missing. The missing letters make a proper three-letter word on
> their own. Write the three-letter word.

Example

She spread the sweet HY on her toast.   <u>ONE</u>

9. He got soaked in the sudden DPOUR. _____

10. The TNAMENT included all of the teams. _____

11. The actor gave a most DATIC performance of the part. _____

12. You must remember to use PARAPHS in your writing! _____

13. The public TSPORT was very efficient, and always on time. _____

14. Please see the nurse in the TRMENT room for a new dressing. _____   /6

> In each of these sentences, there is a four-letter word hidden across two words. The letters are in the right order and make a correctly spelt word. Write the word.

Example

It was fis<u>h and</u> chips for supper.   <u>hand</u>

15. She chose her favourite colours for the cushions. _____

16. He travelled so far every day. _____

17. She found her apron lying on the floor. _____

18. Come and see us as soon as you can. _____

19. I must collect our tickets today. _____   /6

20. Put that bunch in the bucket over there. _____

> Remove one letter from the word in capitals to leave a new word. The meaning of the new word is given in the clue.

Example

WANT   an insect   <u>ANT</u>

21. SPORT   classify   _____

22. RAFTER   later   _____

23. FLOUNDER   originator   _____

24. SLIGHT   ability to see _____

25. COMPOSER   write music   _____   /6

26. COMMA   unconscious   _____

77

Rearrange the capital letters to form a correctly spelt word that will complete these sentences sensibly. Write the word on the answer line.

Example

She led the horse to the ABTESL.   <u>STABLE</u>

27. They each carried their own UKCACSRK on the trek. _____

28. The old TERNLNA by the door lit up the dark driveway. _____

29. The captain was always ITOIPVSE and full of encouragement. _____

30. She enjoyed using her new MECARA on the trip. _____

31. The children had six different SESLNSO each day. _____

32. The extinct LAONVOC had a distinctive shape. _____

/6

Move one letter from the first word and add it to the second word, to make two new, correctly spelt words. The order of the letters **cannot** be changed.

Example

plain   pad   →   <u>plan</u>   <u>paid</u>

33. tripe   bat   →   _____   _____

34. flank   nit   →   _____   _____

35. beach   ale   →   _____   _____

36. scamper   lice   →   _____   _____

37. snail   cat   →   _____   _____

38. gasp   anthers   →   _____   _____

/6

Look carefully at the first two pairs of words, and then complete the third pair in the same way.

Example

cat, cart   ten, tern   ban, ?   <u>barn</u>

39. pin, pine   spin, spine   win, _____

40. ringing, ringer   flinging, flinger   singing, _____

41. moat, mat   skip, sip   chop, _____

42. fellow, flow   barrow, brow   sallow, _____

43. tingle, tug   jingle, jug   mingle, _____

44. saw, was   drab, bard   stab, _____   /6

Substitute the values for the letters and work out these equations. Give each answer as a letter.

Example

If A = 2, B = 5, C = 8, D = 12 and E = 20, what is the value of A $\times$ E $\div$ C = ?   <u>B</u>

If A = 2, B = 6, C = 8, D = 18 and E = 22, what is the value of:

45. D + B $-$ A = _____

46. A $\times$ C + B = _____

47. E $-$ C + B $-$ A = _____

If A = 4, B = 10, C = 2, D = 14 and E = 30, what is the value of:

48. B $\times$ C + A $-$ D = _____

49. C $\times$ D + C = _____   /6

50. A $\times$ B $\div$ C + B = _____

/50

PAPER 18

Look carefully at these letter sequences. Work out the patterns to find the next letters in each sequence. Write them on the answer line. The alphabet is here to help you.

A B C D E F G H I J K L M N O P Q R S T U V W X Y Z

Example

AB	DE	GH	JK	?	<u>MN</u>

1. DE   ZY   FG   XW   _____

2. EH   YV   HK   VS   KN   _____

3. AU   BW   CY   DA   _____

4. TR   PN   LJ   HF   _____

5. ZM   YN   XO   WP   _____

6. AB   CE   FI   JN   _____

/6

Substitute the values for the letters and work out these equations. Give each answer as a letter.

Example

If $A = 2$, $B = 5$, $C = 8$, $D = 12$ and $E = 20$, what is the value of $A \times E \div C = ?$ <u>B</u>

If $A = 15$, $B = 30$, $C = 3$, $D = 10$ and $E = 2$, what is the value of:

7. $D + C + E =$ _____

8. $A \times C - B =$ _____

9. $D + C + E + B - A =$ _____

If A = 12, B = 4, C = 18, D = 24 and E = 3, what is the value of:

10. C ÷ E + A = _____

11. D ÷ E + B = _____

/6

12. A + D ÷ E + E + E = _____

> Which of the following words **cannot** be made from the letters of the word in capitals? Underline the word.

Example

STATIONERY   state   stone   <u>towns</u>   notes   train

13. PRINCIPLE   prince   price   spine   nicer   nipper

14. CAPITAL   tail   clap   plait   place   pit

15. RECIPE   riper   rice   creep   price   pier

16. SERRATED   trade   tears   steer   steed   treat

17. CARAMEL   mare   cream   clam   meal   cereal

/6

18. SHOWER   show   who   wish   rows   shoe

> Write these words into the grid so that they can be read across and down the grid.

Example

TOP   TIN   NAY   PAY

T	O	P
I		A
N	A	Y

19. DIP   SUM   MAP   SAD

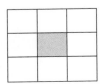

20. ERE   ATE   EAT
      BEE   OAR   BOA

/2

In each group of five words below, there are three words that go together in some way. Identify the two words that **do not** belong to the group and underline them.

Example

cat   <u>cockerel</u>   donkey   camel   <u>python</u>

21. shrimp   moth   eel   shark   spider

22. herd   alone   school   solitary   flock

23. feather   fur   beak   claw   scales

24. agate   emerald   clay   quartz   silt

25. trek   stamp   boots   trail   track

26. glass   pan   tumbler   beaker   dish

/6

Look carefully at the given codes and work out the answers to the questions.

Example

If the code for STEAM is 32415, what does the code 341 stand for?   <u>SEA</u>

If the code for RAMBLE is 246135:

27. What is the code for LAMB? _____

28. What does the code 6543 stand for? _____

29. What is the code for REAL? _____

If the codes for DIP, DEN and PIN are 135, 124 and 534, but not in that order:

30. What is the code for DINE? _____

31. What does the code 535 stand for? _____

32. What is the code for PENNED? _____

/6

Move one letter from the first word and add it to the second word, to make two new, correctly spelt words. The order of the letters **cannot** be changed.

Example

plain   pad   →   <u>plan</u>   <u>paid</u>

33. freight   car   → _____ _____

34. stomp   cap   → _____ _____

35. fleet   best   → _____ _____

36. swing   dies   → _____ _____

37. craters   bought   → _____ _____

38. flint   bag   → _____ _____

/6

In each sentence below, the word in capitals has three letters missing. The missing letters make a proper three-letter word on their own. Write the three-letter word.

Example

She spread the sweet HY on her toast.   <u>ONE</u>

39. Her favourite history IC was the Romans. _____

40. The BET was full of harvest gifts. _____

41. Her mum BRUD her long hair carefully. _____

42. He bit into the apple with a loud CCH. _____

43. He had gone but no one saw him DISAPR. _____

44. The couple were WALG hand in hand along the shore. _____

/6

Add one letter from the word in capitals to make a new word. The meaning of the new word is given in the clue.

Example

ANT   desire   <u>WANT</u>

45. WINE   pigs   _____

46. LOCKED   impassable   _____

47. COUNTY   rural   _____

48. CAMPED   little room   _____

49. HALLOW   not deep   _____

50. EDGE   rush-like plant _____

/6

/50

PAPER 19

Look carefully at the given codes and work out the answers to the questions.

Example

If the code for STEAM is 32415, what does the code 341 stand for?   <u>SEA</u>

If the code for PASTE is 12345:

1. What is the code for STEP? _____

2. What does the code 1524 stand for? _____

3. What is the code for TAPS? _____

If the codes for TEN, BIN and BEE are 233, 214 and 534, but not in that order:

4. What is the code for BENT? _____

5. What does the code 415 stand for? _____

6. What is the code for BITE? _____

/6

> Choose two words, one from each set of brackets, so that the second pair of words is completed in the same way as the first pair.

Example

Cow is to (milk, <u>calf,</u> herd) as horse is to (jump, saddle, <u>foal</u>).

7. Yellow is to (paint, butter, sunshine) as red is to (cherry, pen, lips).

8. Spoon is to (soup, ladle, pudding) as knife is to (carve, blade, sharp).

9. Fanfare is to (royalty, music, trumpet) as foghorn is to (coastline, lighthouse, noise).

10. Tailor is to (fabric, suit, measurement) as tanner is to (stitching, leather, sunshine).

11. Internet is to (games, computer, studying) as encyclopaedia is to (library, alphabet, volume).

12. Hours is to (minutes, clock, time) as miles is to (roads, distance, kilometres).

/6

> Remove one letter from the word in capitals to leave a new word. The meaning of the new word is given in the clue.

Example

WANT   an insect   <u>ANT</u>

13. BANGLE   corner   _____

14. CAMBER   orange   _____

15. DIRECTORY   of a film   _____

16. ENVOY   jealousy   _____

17. FINALE   the last   _____

/6

18. GUILT   gold edged _____

Put these words into the grid so that they can be read going across or going down the grid.

Example

TOP   TIN   NAY   PAY

19. BED   ODD   COO
CAB   ODE   ADD

20. WIG   ACE   NET
WAN   ICE   GET

/2

In each sentence below, the word in capitals has three letters missing. The missing letters make a proper three-letter word on their own. Write the three-letter word.

Example

She spread the sweet HY on her toast.   <u>ONE</u>

21. The PAR was very talkative. _____

22. The FER bought a new tractor. _____

23. On the prairies, they have vast herds of TLE. _____

24. The river MEERED across the plain to the sea. _____

25. The driver was rushed into HOSAL after the accident. _____

26. The last person to OCY this house left over a year ago. _____

/6

Move one letter from the first word and add it to the second word, to make two new, correctly spelt words. The order of the letters **cannot** be changed.

Example

plain   pad   →   <u>plan</u>   <u>paid</u>

27. whine   core   →   _____   _____

28. shred   pot   →   _____   _____

29. faction   rat   →   _____   _____

30. praised   was   →   _____   _____

31. flock   lap   →   _____   _____

32. simile   ran   →   _____   _____

/6

Look carefully at these letter sequences. Work out the patterns to find the next letters in the sequence. The alphabet is here to help you.

A B C D E F G H I J K L M N O P Q R S T U V W X Y Z

Example

AB   DE   GH   JK   ?   <u>MN</u>

33. MC   ND   OE   PF   _____

34. ZY   BA   XW   DC   VU   _____

35. AD   BE   CF   DG   _____

36. LM   KN   JO   IP   _____

37. VA   WB   XC   YD   _____

38. AA   AC   BE   BG   CI   _____

/6

87

Rearrange the capital letters to form a correctly spelt word that will complete these sentences sensibly. Write the word on the answer line.

Example

She led the horse to the ABTESL.   <u>STABLE</u>

39. Her SEMHTAR was active all night, running in its cage. _____

40. They collected loads of SISFOLS along the pebble beach. _____

41. The original MRUSCATNIP was kept at the museum. _____

42. The children were learning their ISONSOPIT on the pitch. _____

43. The sea birds EDIVD effortlessly for the fish. _____

44. The Milky Way is our nearest ALXAYG. _____

/6

Which of the following words **cannot** be made from the letters of the word in capitals? Underline the word.

Example

STATIONERY   state   stone   <u>towns</u>   notes   train

45. GALLEON   gale   alone   along   longer   angel

46. IMITATE   team   time   meet   mate   meat

47. LOUNGE   gun   long   gong   lone   glue

48. MESSAGE   sage   amiss   games   seams   gases

49. MINSTREL   mines   reins   strain   tries   limes

50. NURSERY   runs   urn   user   sure   sunny

/6

/50

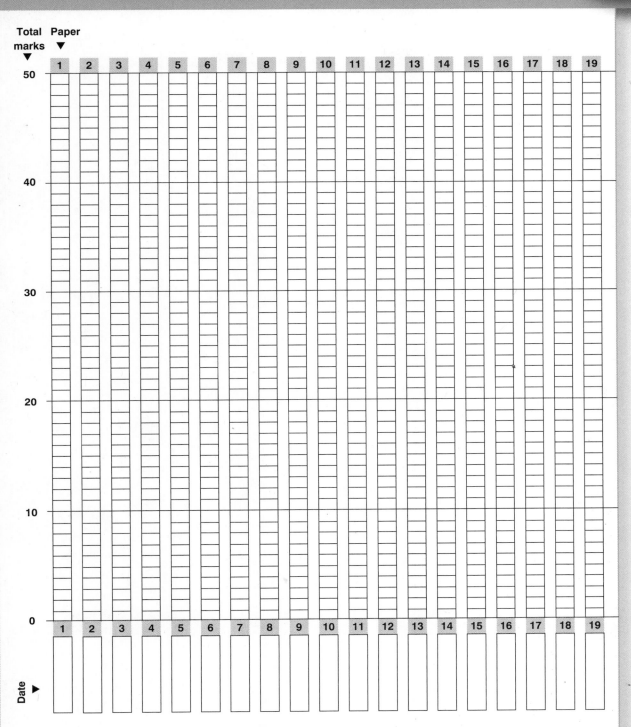

Now colour in your score!

Notes